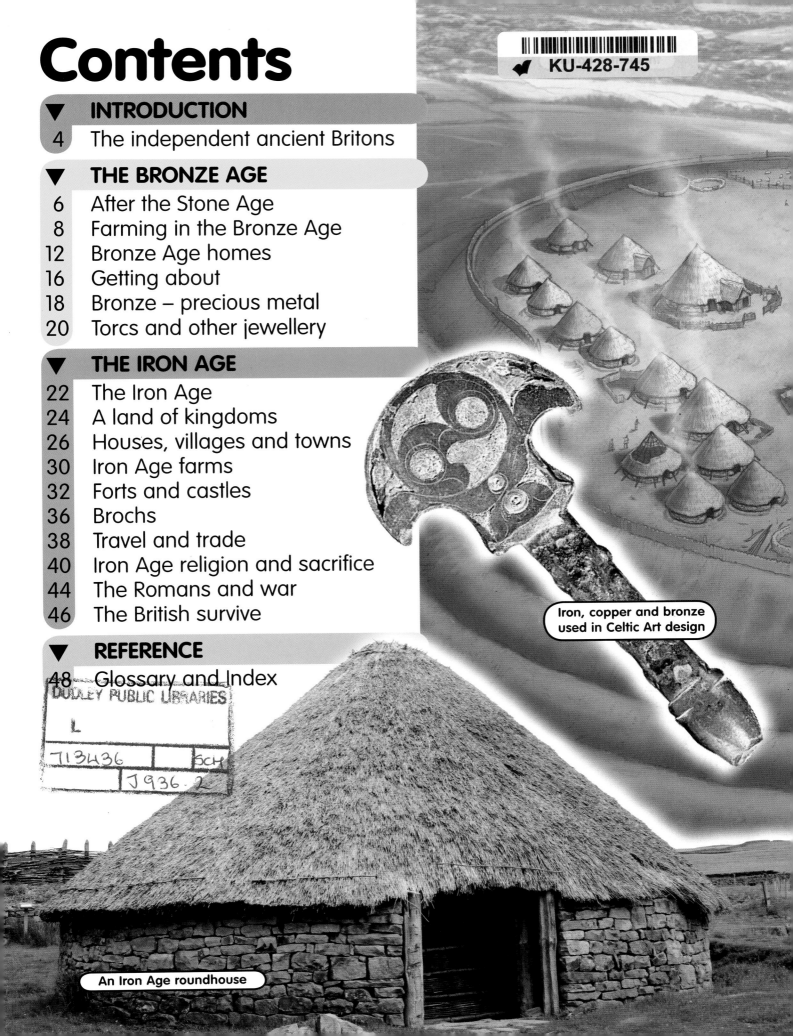

Contents

Iron, copper and bronze used in Celtic Art design

An Iron Age roundhouse

The independent ancient Britons

This book is about the British who lived between Bronze Age times and the arrival of the Saxons and Vikings. These are ancestors to most of us who live in Britain even today.

We are going to look at a long lost time following the Stone Age. Archaeologists generally call this the time of the **ANCIENT BRITONS**. It began in the **BRONZE AGE** and continued through the **IRON AGE**. This is also the time when, on the mainland of Europe, one of the most powerful groups of people were the **CELTS**.

You will find that there is remarkably little left that was made by the ancient Britons of this time, and much of what we know about what life was like comes from writings of the ancient Greeks and Romans, who also lived during the Bronze and Iron Ages.

The Greeks and the Romans divided up the peoples in northern and western Europe into the Britons, the Celts, the Germans and the Iberians (Spain and Portugal). Notice that they did not call the Britons Celts. But the peoples of Britain and the Celts did share many things, because they traded together. As a result, many Britons spoke a form of Celtic language and developed the same kind of art.

People in Britain also traded with the Germans, and this had an effect in the

Curriculum Visions

Celtic times

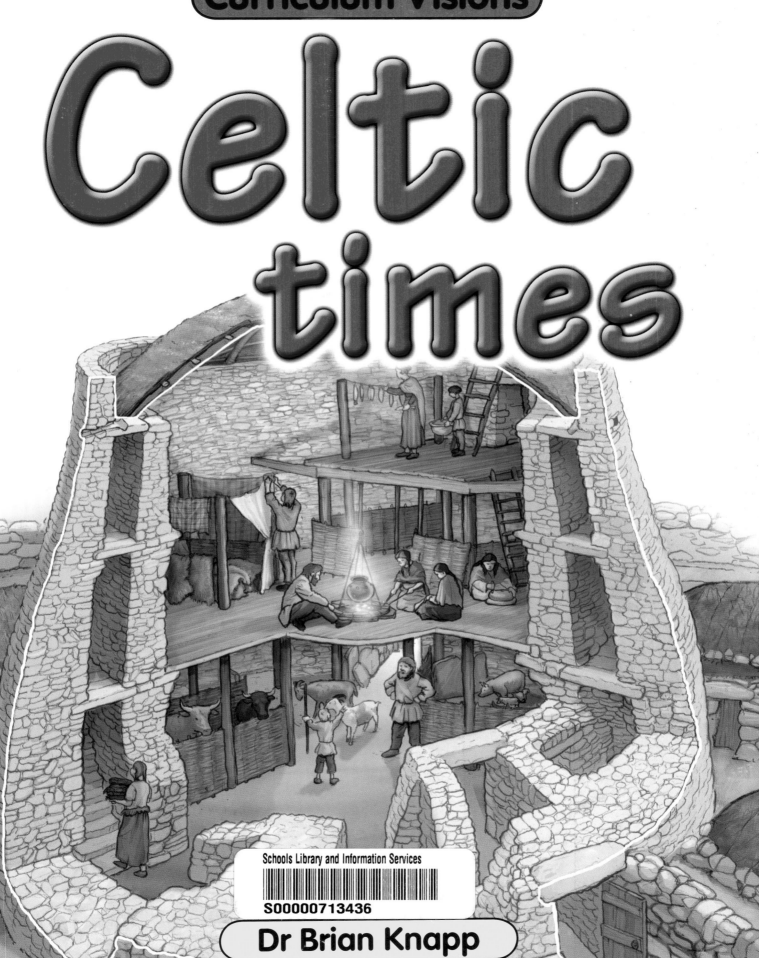

Dr Brian Knapp

Bronze Age farming

Swirling Celtic Art designs on a harness

Curriculum Visions

There's much more on-line including videos

You will find multimedia resources covering a wide range of topics in the Professional Zone at:

www.CurriculumVisions.com

A CVP Book © Earthscape 2008

Author
Brian Knapp, BSc, PhD

Senior Designer
Adele Humphries, BA, PGCE

Editor
Gillian Gatehouse

Designed and produced by
EARTHSCAPE

Printed in China by
WKT Company Ltd

Celtic times – Curriculum Visions
A CIP record for this book is available from the British Library

Paperback ISBN 978 1 86214 572 6

Illustrations
All illustrations by Mark Stacey except the following: David Woodroffe 24–25.

Picture credits
All photographs are from the Earthscape Picture Library except the following (c=centre t=top b=bottom l=left r=right): TopFoto/British Museum 2b, 3c, 18–19, 20, 21, 22–23, 38–39, 40–41, 42–43; ShutterStock 6–7, 36–37 (main).

This product is manufactured from sustainable managed forests. For every tree cut down at least one more is planted.

In this book we shall use the word Britain as a shorthand to mean the British Isles. The break up of the British Isles into its various countries is too recent to have any meaning during Celtic times.

south and east, too, bringing an early form of 'Saxon' language with them. But although invasion was commonplace in Europe, no-one invaded Britain. The **ANCESTORS** of the people who lived in Britain at the end of the Iron Age were still the peoples who had arrived after the Ice Age, together with a few refugees and people who had come to set up business – a sort of mixture like today.

Were they British?

It's easy to think of being part of a nation today, as we have lots of ways of knowing about the place we call home. But that is partly because we have good ways of knowing about it: TV, books and so on. People in the Bronze and Iron Ages did not travel about, except locally, so they would not have thought of themselves as British at all, but simply members of a **TRIBE** or **KINGDOM**. But neighbouring tribes/kingdoms did have lots in common. So it's from our view of being able to see what was going on in the whole country that we can group these people together as 'ancient Britons' (picture ①). They would no more have used the term Briton than the word Celt.

Year	BRONZE AGE
2200 BC	Bronze Age begins in Britain
2000 BC	Extraction of copper ore begins in British Isles
1900 BC	The final part of Stonehenge is begun
1500 BC	The first fields
1350 BC	Wooden boatbuilding at Dover
1100 BC	First hilltop settlements
Year	IRON AGE
800 BC	Iron-working comes to Britain
600–100 BC	Main time of 'hillfort' and broch building
500 BC	Celtic Art
80 BC	The first gold coins minted in Britain
55 and 54 BC	Julius Caesar's invasions into Britain
AD 43	Roman invasion army arrives at Richborough (Kent)
AD 45	Romans quickly take control of south eastern England, but this only affects the British nobles, not the farmers
AD 61	Boudicca of the Iceni leads a rebellion but is defeated by Roman forces
AD 78	Agricola begins to invade Scotland
AD 122	Hadrian's Wall
AD 142	Antonine Wall
AD 350–369	Romans abandon Scotland
AD 400	Hadrian's Wall abandoned
AD 410	The Romans leave and the Saxons begin to take over control of England

BRONZE AND IRON AGE (including ROMAN) TIMELINE

▼ ② **An Iron Age pot reconstructed by archaeologists.**

People who study this time are known as archaeologists. They get their information by interpreting the things that ancient people left behind and which are often found by excavation (picture ②).

People who study written records to find out what went on in the past are called historians.

The period we are dealing with has a bit of both. The people of Britain did not write anything down, and so most of what they did has to be found out from archaeology. But the Greeks and Romans did describe the ancient Britons, and what they said is found out from historical records.

◄ ① **An Iron Age Briton at the time of the Roman invasion – a simple farmer, as he had been for thousands of years.**

5

Weblink: www.CurriculumVisions.com

After the Stone Age

Stonehenge was begun in the Stone Age and finished in the early Bronze Age. Then all such circles were abandoned because they had no further use.

The earliest time in history is called the Stone Age. There were not many people about in the Stone Age (for more details see the Curriculum Visions book *'The Stone Age'*), but they did some remarkable things such as build great stone circles like the one at Drumbeg (picture ①) and Stonehenge.

However, about 4,200 years ago people in Britain learned about making the metal called bronze. It changed their lives. For historians this marks the end of the Stone Age and the start of the Bronze Age. But, at first, bronze was not widely used. It took time to make its mark. That is why most people carried on doing what they had done in the Stone Age, including finishing off building Stonehenge.

▶ ① **This stone circle at Drumbeg in Ireland, like all other stone circles in the British Isles, now sits among fields, an abandoned ruin since Bronze Age times.**

A land of farmers

Most of the people in the Stone Age had been hunters of wild animals and gatherers of roots, berries and other foods that grew naturally. But that is not a very efficient way of using the land. Just a few people need a huge territory to give them enough food. So as the number of people grew, it became impossible to carry on that way. Groups of people soon began to set out hunting territories for themselves and then began to turn to farming, learning it from neighbours on the continent.

While people were HUNTER-GATHERERS, they just needed some places to meet from time to time, and the stone circles gave them that. But farming changes everything. It makes people stay in one place, and so great seasonal meetings are not possible. Farmers also looked at the world differently from wanderers and they changed the way they thought of their gods. So they abandoned the stone circles forever. By the middle of the Bronze Age people were making fields all over the spirit lands around Stonehenge, just as they were elsewhere. Stone Age ideas were dead.

Farming in the Bronze Age

People began to settle down to farming at the end of the Stone Age and early Bronze Age.

You may be expecting to see pictures of great monuments built during Bronze Age times. After all, if people could make great stone circles in the Stone Age, shouldn't they have made something bigger in the Bronze Age? Well, they didn't. You see, the people of the Stone Age were largely wanderers, getting food was easy, and they had time on their hands. They used this time to make great monuments and build barrows. They did all that with less than a quarter of a million people in the entire British Isles.

The treadmill of farming

Farming uses up your time in a totally different way. It ties you to the small patch of land you are working. You don't have time for seasonal wandering, and you don't all gather in one place to do massive things. It is probably this change that made people change their religion, too.

If your religion has changed, the monuments would seem useless things. So the Bronze Age people dug ditches, made banks, and created fields in which to keep their little animals (Bronze Age cows and other animals were much smaller than the ones we have today, like the brown Soay sheep, picture ①).

Where people farmed

Britain had not, however, been turned into farmland overnight. Farming was patchy. Some people chose hilly areas like Dartmoor (picture ③ pages 10–11) and Salisbury Plain, where the forests were easier to clear than the valleys. Some chose the edges of lakes and fens.

Of course, farming was very primitive and this is what made it time-consuming. For example, a dibber was used to make a hole in which to drop seed.

▶ ① A Soay sheep.

Forest was still everywhere around. So these early farmers worked the land, then popped into the forest from time to time to see if they could bag a wild deer. Life was still a mixture of farming and hunting.

New ideas

New revolutionary ideas were reaching our Bronze Age ancestors. One of the greatest ideas was making cloth by spinning and weaving wool. The Stone Age people made their clothes from skins. But the Bronze Age people spun wool, and wove cloth.

Loom frames were made with branches lashed up into a square, and the long strands of wool were kept under tension by tying little discs of stone to the lower ends (picture ②). The horizontal strands of wool thread were then woven in and out of the stretched threads and pushed tightly together using long-toothed combs made of animal bone.

Wrap-around clothing

At this stage people probably simply took the square of cloth that came off the loom, and which looked like a blanket, and wrapped it around themselves, tying it up with some kind of string and fixing it with brooches. But it was a huge step forward.

The growth of skills

Farmers needed to make almost everything they wanted. So they made cloth in their roundhouses, gouged out wood into bowls, spoons and so on.

Yet there were some things that everyday farmers could not make successfully for themselves. Pot-making needs skill and this is why pots were traded. Of course the things most precious and widely traded of all, were the items made of bronze: axe heads, hoe heads, daggers and the like.

What could they be bought with? Sheep, cattle and any other tiny surplus the farmer might be able to spare once every few years.

Old ideas

People don't simply give up old ways just because they have learnt new ones. They add the new ones to the old ones. So although the priests no longer used stone circles, the idea of religion, shrines and priests did not go away, as we shall see.

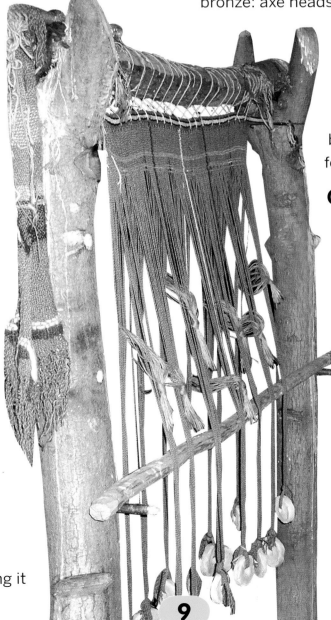

◄ ② A reconstructed Bronze Age weaving loom.

Woollen clothes and hat

Small fields with boundary banks or ditches

Animals were much smaller than those we have today

▼ ③ Upland farmers, such as those living on Dartmoor, would have been quite isolated and in much smaller communities than in some other places. Working the stony soil would also have given very different kinds of farms from working the lowland fens.

Gently-sloping roofs of roundhouses

Antlers for hoes and ploughs

Bronze Age homes

Bronze Age people started a new fashion in house-building – round homes.

Life in the Bronze Age was tough. It was also short. In this kind of world it made sense to get 'married' fast, and to have lots of children. Many of those children would die young from disease, but if you had a big family, some children would survive to help with the farm and other chores, and to look after their parents when they were too worn out to continue (perhaps when they were in their 30s!).

In these times, people did not live in small families as we do today, but as a community of related people. This meant that each little farm was a mass of children and adults, as well as the animals that were kept in the home over night and away from wolves.

The roundhouse

You needed quite a bit of space for all those family members and animals. In the Stone Age, people had built rectangular houses (and they continued to do this on the continent) but, for some reason we do not know, the fashion in Britain changed from square to round houses (pictures ①, ②, and ③ on pages 14–15).

A typical house was 10 m or so across. That's big – big enough to get a couple of dozen people in.

Roundhouses are quite easy to build using materials to hand, namely young tree stems, mud, straw and a dose of cattle dung.

Nevertheless, a house needed to be built strongly. A roof could be heavy (several tonnes) when wet, as it was made using turf, not the lightweight thatch we shall see used in the Iron Age. The roof angle could not be steep, either, or the turf would slip off.

▼ ① **A reconstruction of a Bronze Age house.**

▼ ② **Inside a Bronze Age house.**

Posts and rafters

To hold the roof rigid, lots of radiating timbers were lashed to two circles of timbers. The result was a kind of cobweb of rafters.

An outer ring of upright posts was used to support the outer part of the roof and possibly provide some sort of 'eaves'. This was also used as a frame on which branches (**WATTLE**) and mud (**DAUB**) could be fixed to make the walls. A second ring of posts stood near the middle of the house and helped prop up the roof near the centre.

Roofs shed a lot of water when it rained, so many homes had a drainage channel dug in the soil below the roof edge to keep water away from the house.

Lighting

There was no hole in the roof to let the smoke out from the fire (because that would have let the heat out and the rain in!) and there were no windows to provide any light. The only light would have come through the south-facing door, and from the fire in the middle of the room.

What people used

It is likely that everyone slept on heather or straw strewn on the floor. By the Bronze Age wool was being woven, and so people were able to sleep covered with blankets rather than the hides that Stone Age people would have used. They may even have put blankets on the straw to make a kind of overnight mattress.

Otherwise, people most likely sat on little wooden stalls and cooked using a large pot that sat more or less permanently on the fire, tenderising the stews that were the main meals of the Bronze Age folk.

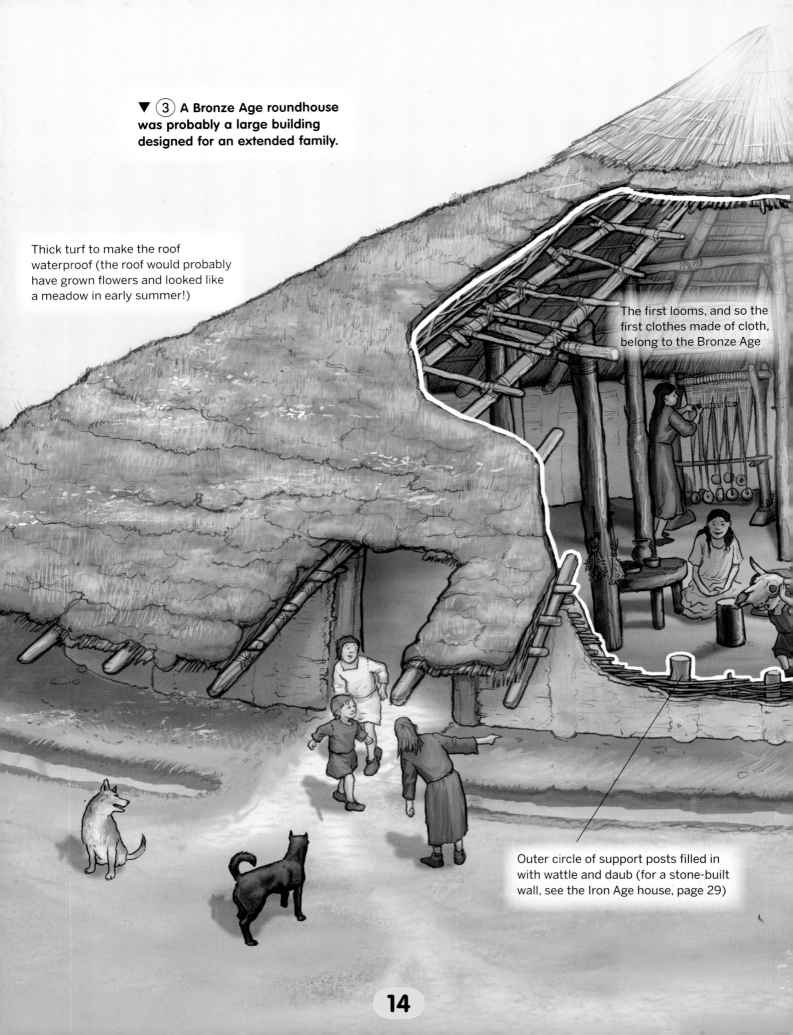

▼ ③ A Bronze Age roundhouse was probably a large building designed for an extended family.

Thick turf to make the roof waterproof (the roof would probably have grown flowers and looked like a meadow in early summer!)

The first looms, and so the first clothes made of cloth, belong to the Bronze Age

Outer circle of support posts filled in with wattle and daub (for a stone-built wall, see the Iron Age house, page 29)

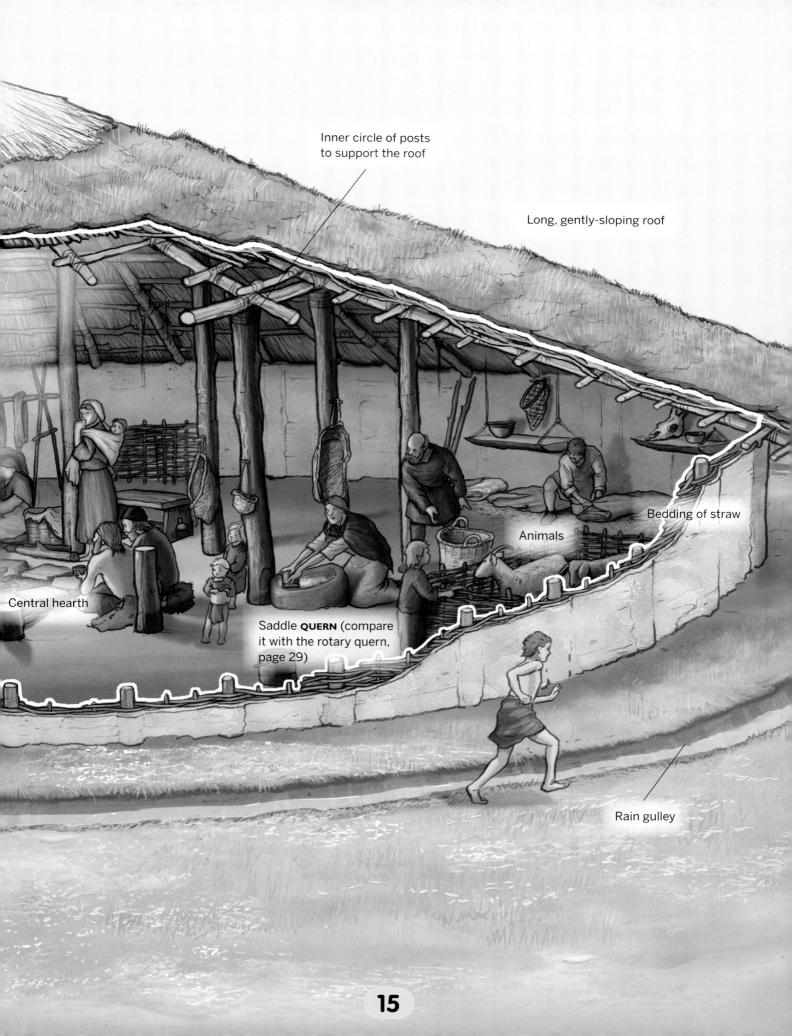

Inner circle of posts
to support the roof

Long, gently-sloping roof

Bedding of straw

Animals

Central hearth

Saddle **QUERN** (compare
it with the rotary quern,
page 29)

Rain gulley

Getting about

The Bronze Age was a time of trade when people made the world's first sea-going boats.

People didn't go far in the Bronze Age. They spent nearly all their time on their farms. But some people took goods from place to place for trade. How did they do this? They could have used pack animals, they could have used carts, or they could use boats.

Carts

The first carts were made at the end of the Stone Age, but they became more common in the Bronze Age. They were small, just about a metre wide, but that was enough for a couple of people or one person and perhaps a small amount of goods. They were used to carry things about the farm, not between places, for there were no good tracks.

Boats

Without roads, if people wanted to get about they used boats.

Most everyday boats were either small canoes dug out of a natural tree trunk with an **ADZE**, or **CORACLES** made by stretching hides over a frame of young tree stems. They could only carry a single person and a few goods. So how did they trade long distances, or trade with people on the continent? They needed much bigger and sturdier boats.

The Dover boat

The remains of one of the world's oldest seagoing boats – 3,550 years old, and so

The finished sea-worthy boat being rowed away

a Bronze Age boat – has been found near Dover. It is 15 m long and 2.4 m wide. The boat was made of two flat-bottom planks, four side-planks and two end-planks.

This is a much bigger boat than could be made by digging out a large tree trunk. In fact, it needed the timber from three trees. So how was it made?

To begin with, two parts were hollowed out of a tree (picture ①). These would make part of the sides and floor of the boat.

▼ ① Making a Bronze Age boat

Making a sea-going boat from a number of trees

Normal dug-out boat

Then, thick planks were cut from another tree. However, at this time they did not have nails, so how did they fasten the pieces of boat together? The flat-bottom planks were held together with long wooden bars and wedges. The extra side planks were 'stitched' together using thick, pliable yew twigs, and the joints were stuffed with moss, wax and resin to make the boat watertight.

The boat builders used bronze axes, adzes, chisels and gouges – they could not have done this before bronze was invented.

When finished, the boat would have been manned by at least 18 oarsmen. It was big enough to carry more people, goods and even animals. Its importance was that goods and ideas could now easily be passed between Europe and Britain, although you would have had to wait for calm seas before you set out across the Channel in this over-sized row-boat!

Bronze – precious metal

The Bronze Age was named after the invention of making bronze – a gold-coloured, but hard metal that could be made into axes and other things.

The Bronze Age gets its name from the first time people worked with bronze, a mixture of copper and tin. But you should not think bronze was widely used. At the start of the Bronze Age it was extremely rare and even by the end of the Bronze Age it was only used for valuable things such as tools and weapons. For everything else there was stone, pottery, bone and wood!

▲▼▶ (1) British Bronze Age ritual gifts to the gods: **1** a sickle (used for harvesting corn); **2** a socketed axe; **3** an axe; **4** a spearhead; and **5** a socketed spearhead.

Mining

In the early Bronze Age people still dug with antlers. So you might think that they could do very little. But you would be wrong. In the north of Wales there is a huge mine called Great Orme. It was dug into the mountains in the Bronze Age and its purpose was to mine copper, a soft, orangy-coloured rock. The miners there dug into the rock using antlers for shovels and they eventually got out about 250 tonnes of copper!

Bronze is hard and it doesn't easily break. Flint axes, on the other hand, quickly break. Bronze can also be cast into whatever shape you want (picture ①), so it saved a lot of time and effort compared to shaping flints (see the Curriculum Visions companion book 'The Stone Age').

Recycling

Because copper and tin were difficult to get from the ground, and they were not easy to turn into bronze, the things people made with bronze were not thrown away lightly. If they were used for axes or hoes, for example, they would have been melted down and reused whenever they became worn out. This is why we do not see many ordinary, worn out bronze items.

Offerings

Curiously, most of the bronze items in museums are in almost perfect condition. Why should this be? It is probably because, in the Bronze Age, people started to make offerings to their gods of the things most precious to them: things made of bronze.

They seem to have offered different types of things in different places. They placed weapons like fine swords and shields in lakes, and rivers. They buried jewellery in the ground. So what you see in museums are items that were never used, nor meant to be used. Their purpose was simply to please the gods.

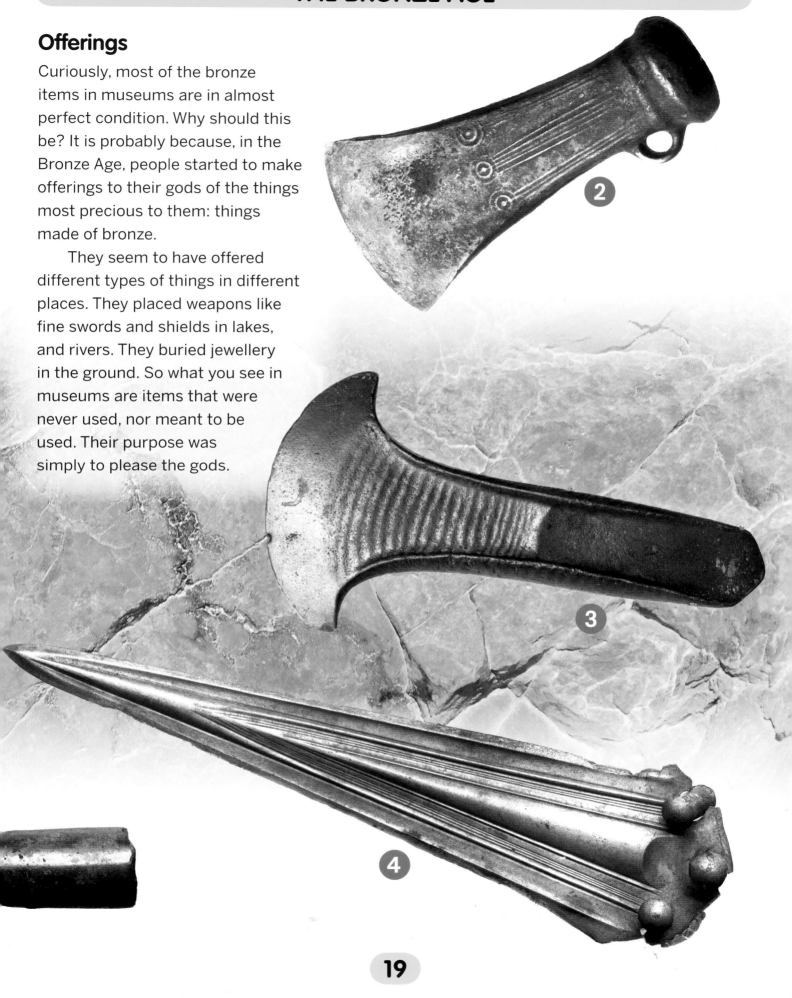

Torcs and other jewellery

The most famous piece of jewellery from before Roman times is a neckband called a torc.

People had learned to work with gold and silver long before they learned to work with bronze. But gold and silver cannot be used for tools and weapons because they are too soft. Nevertheless, the way they shine makes them attractive metals to own. This is why gold and silver have nearly always been used for jewellery.

The **TORC** is the most famous piece of gold and silver jewellery made in prehistory (pictures ① and ②). It is a neckband made sometimes out of solid metal, but more often out of wires of metal twisted together. The word torc comes from the Latin for 'to twist'.

If you were to handle a torc, the first thing you would notice is that it cannot easily be bent. The metal is simply too massive. Yet these ornaments were worn around the neck. So it is likely that a torc was fitted to someone (wealthy) when they became an adult and that they never took it off again, much like we might wear a wedding ring today.

Most torcs were made in the Iron Age, which is our next period of history, but torcs were first made in the Bronze Age, and so the torc belongs to both periods.

During the Stone Age people did not seem to want to give things to their gods. Perhaps they did this in the form of food and captured animals, but we do not know. By the Bronze Age, the religion was changing and people started to believe that their gods were all around them in nature. They probably already regarded water and rivers as being special in the Stone Age, but in the Bronze Age, people began to make fine goods just to offer to their water gods, unused bronze swords, bracelets, and neckbands called torcs – some made in solid gold. These special gifts are the things you now see in museums. They were not everyday objects – they were the best that the people could make and offer to their gods.

▶ ① This is part of the earth burial or 'hoard' at Snettisham, Norfolk. The torcs, and bracelets were buried about 75 BC.

▼ ② This torc was made from 64 metal threads, twisted first into groups of eight, then twisted together again.

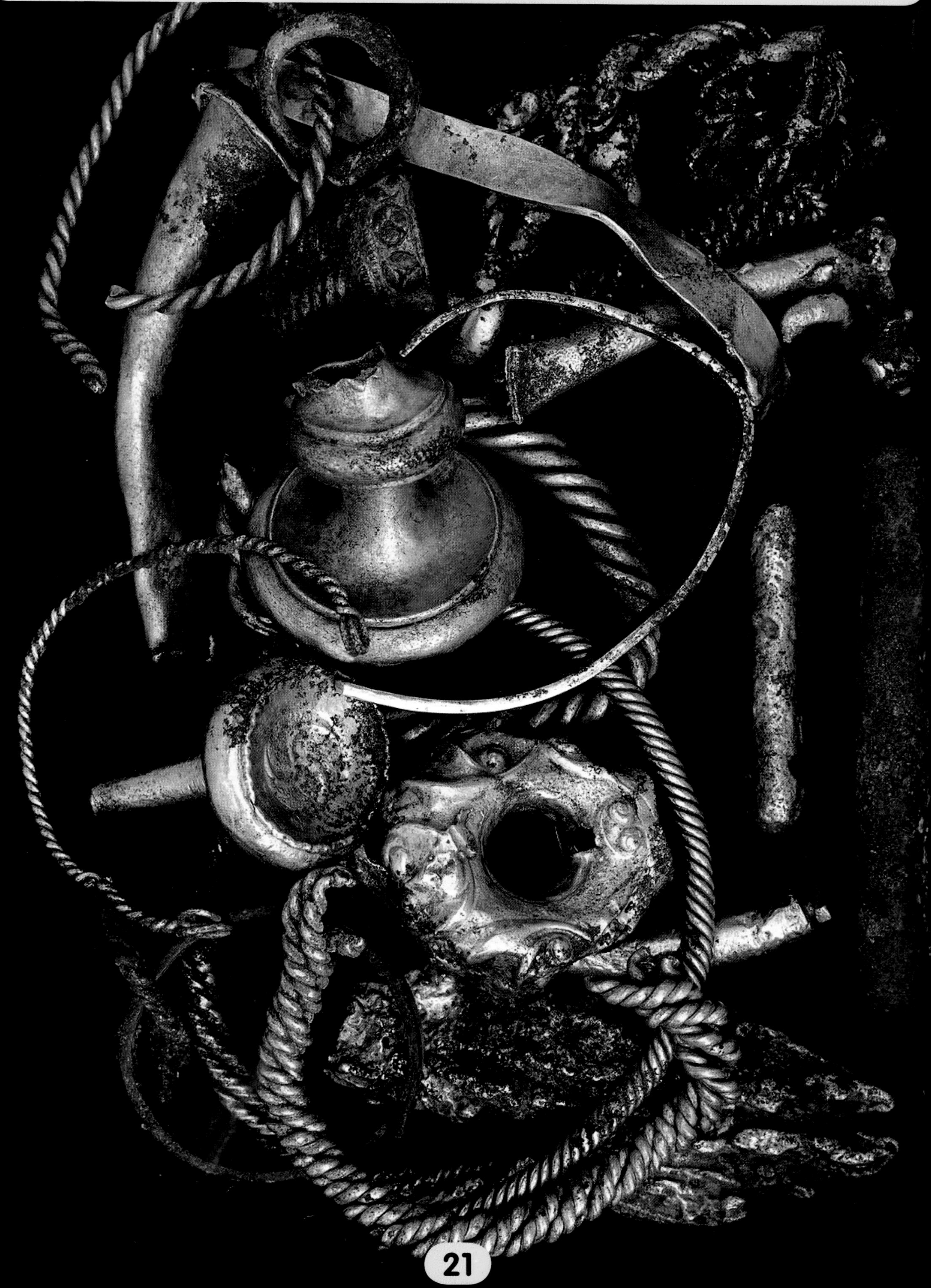

The Iron Age

About 800 BC the knowledge of how to melt and shape iron spread from mainland Europe. It marked the start of the Iron Age, and a very crowded Iron Age, at that.

The Iron Age in Britain started around 800 BC, that is just about 2,800 years ago, and ended in 'England and Wales' with the Roman Conquest.

Iron was first used in what is now Turkey about a thousand years before people in Britain learned how to use it. Even when iron working became known, it was several centuries before iron became the common metal to use for tools. This didn't mean that people stopped using bronze. It was simply that now they were able to use iron where it was more suitable, for example for the tips of ploughs and in swords.

The people of Iron Age Europe were still farmers living on farms, but a few were full-time craftsmen and some lived in sprawling settlements (called oppida, see page 27) and hilltop enclosures (called hillforts, pages 32–35).

A land without writing

Why is it that the Iron Age Britons never made a very dramatic impact on the world, as the ancient Greeks, ancient Egyptians or ancient Romans had done? It may be in part because each of these peoples were city based. Our Iron Age ancestors (who lived at the same time as the Greeks and Romans) felt no real need to gather into

◀▶ ① **What were Britons using at the time of the Roman invasion? Here are finds from a grave. There is a wooden bucket with finely decorated bronze bands holding it together (inset shows detail from the bucket handles), a jug and a cooking pan. These last two items were made in Europe and imported to Britain, showing how common trade was at the time.**

cities – perhaps because the land was good for farming. Also they did not feel that writing was important, while their warriors were not used for empire-building.

So Iron Age Britons built no great towns or cities and wrote down nothing that could be carried on to the present. The Romans and Greeks, on the other hand, developed writing skills. As a result it was they who wrote about the ancient Britons.

What we were like

By looking through the things people left behind in their rubbish dumps and the few burials that we can find (picture ①), it seems that, just as in previous times, people worked hard, often for long periods on their knees grinding corn at a quern, and other chores. As a result, most got arthritis. By the time they were 30 they were old, and soon after they were dead.

Men wore woollen or linen shirts and trousers and women wore blouses, dresses or skirts. During the winter men wore cloaks and women wore shawls. Many wore a neckband (torc) all their lives.

Weblink: www.CurriculumVisions.com

A land of kingdoms

So long as there aren't disasters such as plagues or a famine, populations grow. Growing populations need organising.

At the start of Iron Age times the British Isles might have been home to a third of a million people. By the end of Iron Age times, 700 years later, there were up to two million people. During this short time, extraordinary changes took place.

Gone without a trace

Over the seven centuries of Iron Age times, about 350 generations were born, lived and died – something upwards of fifty million people who left no trace, except for some bits and pieces in their rubbish tips, a scattering of hillforts and the vague lines of fields and houses.

Because they kept no records we don't even know anyone's name. It was foreigners like the Romans who spoke to our Iron Age ancestors and wrote down the names of a few people – mainly kings. It was even the Romans who gave us our name – calling us Britones or Britanni (Britons).

Kingdoms

What difference does it make when the number of people increases? The more people there are, the more each group of people (a tribe or clan we might call them) needs to get from its own territory. The only alternative is to take over someone else's territory. This is why it becomes important to defend land. So in Iron Age times the ancient Britons began to think differently and get organised. Gradually Iron Age Britain became a land of kingdoms (picture ①) and warriors as well as farmers and craftsmen.

During these times, priests also became important people. They were known as the Druids. Druids were politicians as well as priests. As a result, Druids could be very powerful.

▶ ① **This map shows the kingdoms/ tribes of the British Isles at the end of Iron Age times. It was made by a Greek called Ptolemy living in Roman times and the names are Romanised. It was based on hearsay and so may not be completely accurate, like so much of material written by Romans about the ancient Britons.**

There were also people whose job it was to pass on, by means of stories, the folklore from one generation to the next. They were the poets or bards.

Left alone until the Romans came

In Iron Age times our spoken language was probably Celtic, just as it had been for many centuries. But there were big variations, especially in the south and east where we traded with the people who in later times would be called 'Saxons'. Here people picked up much of their language, too.

As we traded with people on the continent we copied useful things from them, such as how to plough with an iron-tipped plough, and we also copied their style of swirling decoration, which we now call **CELTIC ART**.

Some skilled people also came from the continent and brought new designs, too. There were probably also a few refugees, especially when the Romans advanced across Europe. But other than that, no one tried to invade and no one had to be fought off through the whole of Iron Age times – until the Romans.

Wherever the Romans conquered and took charge, historians mark that as the end of the Iron Age times. So soon after AD 43 the Iron Age ended in England and Wales. But it continued in Scotland (where the Romans never could keep control) and Ireland (where they never reached at all) until the arrival of the Vikings some 700 years after that.

Houses, villages and towns

Many people still lived on their own in farmsteads, but now some lived in villages and towns.

Roundhouses were a curious British invention of Bronze Age times. In other parts of Europe people lived in rectangular houses. Farmers in the Iron Age continued the tradition. However, Iron Age people were not 'stick-in-the-muds'. For example, they changed the materials they used for roofs – from heavy waterlogging turf to lighter thatch (picture ①). This meant they were able to build houses with a steeper pitch to their roofs (up to 45°) and this gave more headroom. Also, with a lightweight thatch they did not need a second set of poles inside their homes as Bronze Age people were forced to put up with, so it was easier to move about inside. A rain gully was dug around the edge of each house to get rid of the water running off the roofs. The walls were still built from local materials such as wattle and daub or, if it was more convenient, of stone.

Family roundhouses

Most Iron Age roundhouses were about 5 to 10 metres across, but some were built up to 15 metres across, which is quite as big as the average modern house – except that it was home to more people. Iron Age houses contained extended families, meaning mum, dad and the kids, and also grandparents, aunts, uncles and cousins – perhaps up to 20 or 30 people.

These houses might have lasted about 20 years, but they were obviously not seen in the same way as we see modern houses – something to pass down to our children or to make money and sell. After all, when the thatch and timbers of a roundhouse started to rot, it was just as easy to build a new house as to repair an old one.

▼ ① **A reconstruction Iron Age house. Notice the earth bank and palisade enclosure behind it.**

Villages

Villages in the past were very different from those we are used to today. They were not organised along roads, for there weren't any. They were just built wherever it was convenient. Each house needed a yard and a stockade to keep wild animals out, so there was quite a lot of room between houses (picture ② pages 28–29).

The largest kind of settlement was almost a town (called an oppidum by the Romans when they arrived). The local chief or king would live in one of these larger places as would most of the warriors and their families. This was probably also where many craftsmen worked, making iron weapons and earthenware pots. Because everyone had their own enclosure and farm animals, it was a sprawling affair, giving the impression of being half town, half country.

Camulodunon

At the end of Iron Age times, the largest oppidum, or town, in Britain was Camulodunon, where modern Colchester, Essex, now stands. Its name means "the Fortress of Camulos" (Camulos was a British god of war). It was the capital of the Trinovantes kingdom. It had many banks and ditches, but these simply marked out property boundaries. They were not meant for defence.

Inside the roundhouse

Roundhouses were single-roomed multi-purpose dwellings, just like almost all houses until Tudor times 1,000 years later.

In the centre of the house was the fireplace hearth and oven. The fire was all purpose: giving heat and light as well as for cooking food. There were no windows.

There were probably piles of straw around the side of the room by day and these were brought near the fire at night and used as beds, perhaps with blankets placed over them.

There would be a loom for weaving, equipment for spinning, simple wooden stools and cooking pots.

The usual food was a vegetable stew, porridge or soup. A pot could be placed on the fire for many hours, allowing the poor quality food to tenderise. Then it might be poured into a communal pot from which everyone helped themselves using wooden spoons. There was also a new invention – an iron spit on which meat could be roasted clear of the fire.

Conical roof of stout timbers supported by stone walls or more timbers and daub and wattle infill depending on what was available

Doorway

Thorn fence to enclose the house

Another important item was the quern. This had been invented in the Stone Age, but grinding flour was made far easier in the Iron Age by a new invention: a stone that turned on top of another one. Both were connected with a common shaft and the top one was turned with a handle. It would have saved much of the backbreaking work that a Stone Age saddle quern required. This 'rotary quern' also produced better flour.

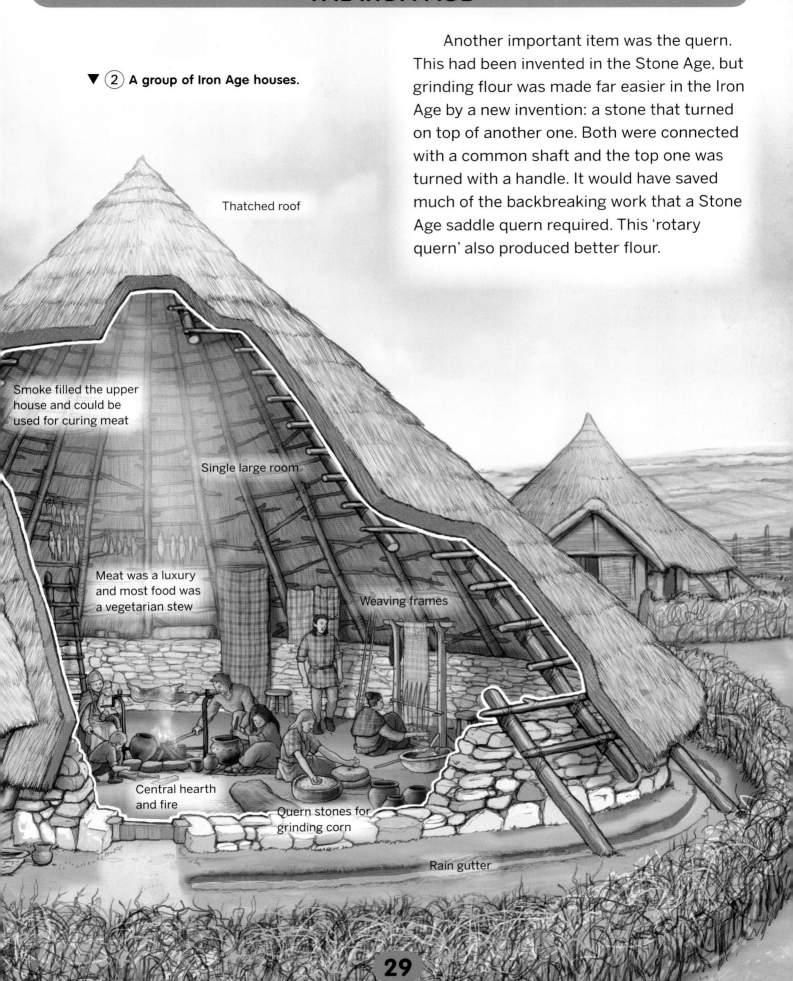

▼ ② **A group of Iron Age houses.**

Thatched roof

Smoke filled the upper house and could be used for curing meat

Single large room

Meat was a luxury and most food was a vegetarian stew

Weaving frames

Central hearth and fire

Quern stones for grinding corn

Rain gutter

Iron Age farms

Farmers had to work hard for their everyday needs. Even then, there was little left over to sell to anyone else.

Almost everyone in Iron Age Britain was a farmer. Most people – including craftsmen and even warriors – would have lived in a farm or small farming village. Farmers had to spend almost all of their time farming just to feed their families.

What happened on a farm

A typical farm had two or three roundhouses and a small farmyard enclosed by a hedge and ditch to keep animals in and wolves out at night.

Most farmers grew wheat and barley, and kept cattle, sheep and pigs, all of which were much smaller than modern breeds – a bit like traditional brown-fleeced Soay sheep (page 8). But new crops, animals, tools and ideas gradually reached these farms from Europe. Beans, cats and chickens were all new to British Iron Age farmers.

Timber was a crop, for wood was needed to make a house, to make tools and to fuel the fire. Many trees were coppiced (cut close to the ground) because this caused the trunk to send up lots of sturdy straight, flexible shoots which were ideal for building with.

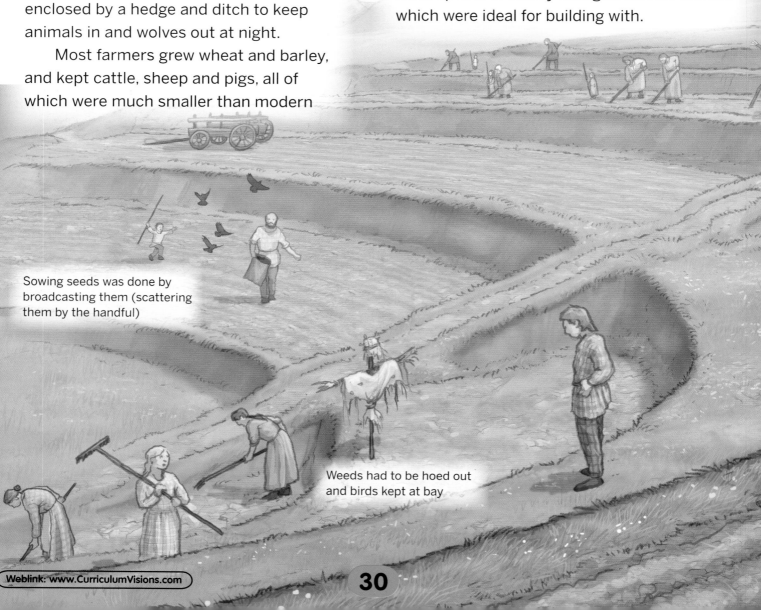

Sowing seeds was done by broadcasting them (scattering them by the handful)

Weeds had to be hoed out and birds kept at bay

During the Iron Age, an iron tip was added to ploughs, making them strong enough to cope with heavy soils.

Strip lynchets

In some places people farmed on slopes because the land was easier to clear than in valley bottoms. As they ploughed, so some of the soil moved downslope. The farmers used this effect to make wide benches, or terraces, across the hillsides. Later they were abandoned and they became grassed over and preserved. Today we know them as strip lynchets (picture ①).

Sidelines

Most people made clothes by weaving them by firelight. But in some places, such as near the sea, there was the chance to make salt and trade it. People living close to sandstone or basalt rocks could make quern stone, those near suitable clay made pots, and those near copper and iron were part-time miners.

▲▼ ① **What hillside farming might have been like in Iron Age times. The small inset photograph shows what these terraces, or strip lynchets, look like today.**

Flat strip of land produced by ploughing across the slope

Iron-tipped plough

Forts and castles

Britain has some of the most impressive hilltop enclosures in Europe. The first historians to look at them thought instantly that they must be forts. But were they right?

▲ ① These banks and ditches (called ramparts) look impressive enough today, after over 2,000 years of decay, but originally the ditches would have had near vertical grassless slopes and the banks would have had rings of wooden posts (palisades) on top. This is Uffington Castle.

So far we have hardly spoken about defence. We have not mentioned forts or castles. This is because people seemed to live quite peaceably without defences until the Iron Age. But everything that is most famous about the Iron Age is supposedly about warfare. I am talking, of course, about the great hilltop 'forts' that you find from southern England to Scotland (picture ②), and also some other quite extraordinary 'castles' – little defended man-made islands in lakes called crannogs, and fortified houses called brochs, that are found in Scotland alone.

The hillforts

If you were to go around Britain a few centuries before the Romans arrived, you would have found a country of three parts. In the east there were some quite sizeable villages of dozens of houses but no sign of defences. If you were to go to the west and north you would have found fewer people, with a few villages surrounded by ring ditches. But, right down the middle of the country, you would have found a land in which people built big enclosures on the tops of hills, the hillforts.

If you visit one – such as at Uffington Castle near Swindon (pictures ① and ③) – you will think they are very impressive indeed. There are rings of ditches with the soil from each ditch made up into banks, or ramparts.

Do you see that I have said enclosure and not fort? Why is this? Because the word fort means something very special – a place simply built for defence in a hostile land. It is true that, in Iron Age times, Britain

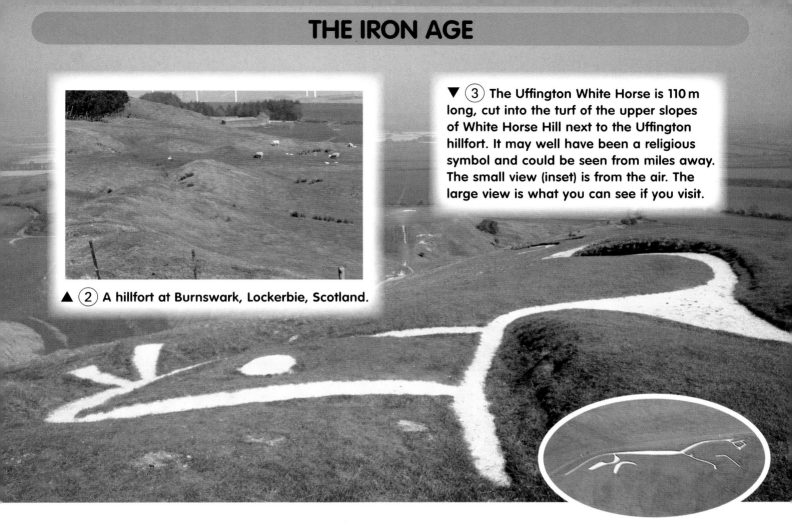

▲ ② A hillfort at Burnswark, Lockerbie, Scotland.

▼ ③ The Uffington White Horse is 110 m long, cut into the turf of the upper slopes of White Horse Hill next to the Uffington hillfort. It may well have been a religious symbol and could be seen from miles away. The small view (inset) is from the air. The large view is what you can see if you visit.

was a land of kingdoms. So it is possible they occasionally needed these places for defence if one kingdom decided to attack another. But actually we don't have any evidence of this. So, supposing they were built for something else, then what could it be? We know that some hundreds of people could live inside them, for they are big and we can find remains of their houses. But it's not a very convenient place to live for day-to-day farming; that would have taken place in the lowlands.

Iron Age palaces?

What was most precious to the ancient Britons? Was it gold or iron? No, it was a supply of grain that would keep you alive over winter. We can find evidence that grain was kept in square buildings on stilts.

It would also be hard for your neighbours to steal your precious grain from these Iron Age 'banks' (picture ④).

Another precious thing would be the temple or shrine to your gods. This, too, might be kept in such a special enclosure.

Whatever kind of defence they might have been needed for as well, they were over-designed. This again suggests to us they might really have been a sign of power, rather like kings in later ages built palaces – places where local kings and family lived and showed off, and in which grain was kept, and fairs held as well. Of course they would have come in handy if the people were attacked.

But hillforts went out of fashion for some reason we don't know and many (but not all) were abandoned before the Romans arrived.

▼ ④ **What an Iron Age hillfort might have looked like. This reconstruction shows you the positions of the central shrine, granaries and houses as well as the ditches and ramparts. It was probably used more like a 'bank' than a fort, and was so well defended it was probably not worth attacking – until the Romans came.**

Granaries were square and on posts and separate from the shrine and houses. They were used to store grain from the surrounding farms.

Pens for animals

Possible chief's house

Shrine to a god

Roundhouses where some people lived

Palisade of wooden stakes, forming a closed fence on top of a ditch

Hillfort on a hilltop with wide views. All the forest from nearby was cleared.

Lowland used for normal farming

Ditches dug and the soil used to make banks, or ramparts

Well to provide water in case of attack

Entrance way, often made like a dog-leg to stop attackers from being able to make a straight charge

Brochs

Scottish brochs were the first stone-built 'castles' in Britain.

In Iron Age times, everyone needed some kind of defence. In places where there were more people, hillforts and cliff-top castles are found. But in parts of the country where there were fewer people, a quite different solution was needed. It also gave us our first true castles – brochs.

Brochs are circular towers with a stairway climbing up between the double walls. They suited the parts of Britain where there were isolated clans, such as in much of Scotland where too much effort would have been needed to make a hillfort. The biggest surviving broch, the Broch of Mousa in the Shetlands (picture ①), was over 14 m tall and made entirely without cement.

It is not clear if the stairway went to the roof, allowing the tower to be used as a lookout, or a place to have thrown down nasty objects on any attackers. But the broch did need quite a lot of people to build it, so it was probably home to the clan leader.

Brochs had several floors, but no windows and the only lighting was from hearths on each floor. Outside the broch were a number of small buildings for storing food and sheltering animals, all enclosed by a further wall. Some brochs were still being lived in until about AD 900.

Main living room

Shelter and protection for animals

Staircase

Double wall

Store rooms and animal shelters

Enclosing wall

◀▲ ① The Broch of Mousa as it is today, and a possible reconstruction of a broch.

Travel and trade

By the Iron Age, the ancient Britons were sharing goods with the continent and speaking much the same language. They were even using coins.

For travel and trade you need three things: a way of getting about, a way of paying for what you want, and a way of talking to other people.

Carts and chariots

Wheeled carts are vital if you are to move goods about on land. Carts made with spoked wheels and iron rims were common in Iron Age times. They had leather straps for springs to make travel more comfortable. They could also be used for carrying warriors, when they were called chariots. Carts and chariots were a sign of wealth and importance so that wheels and even whole chariots were sometimes buried with their owner.

Chariots were greatly feared by the Romans. Chariots, carts, pots, iron weapons, armour and other complicated items needed more skill to make than the average farmer would have had. These, together with tools and boats, were made by full-time craftsmen working in large 'towns' (which the Romans called oppida, see page 27). Often these were also where the British kings lived.

▼ ① Here you see part of a find of 3,000 British-minted silver coins from Iron Age times. They were found buried in the ground. Collections of this kind are called hoards. Notice that they are all dish-shaped and use Latin writing even though the Britons spoke a Celtic language. Writing in Latin was a very prestigious thing to do in Iron Age Britain and gives you an idea who the Britons thought of as the world super-power at the time.

Coins

Coins were invented about 600 BC in what is modern Turkey. They were made by stamping a design onto a small disc of metal. The ancient Britons knew about Greek and Roman coins and copied them (picture ①).

Making coins is a sign of trade, but also a sign of wealth. Many British tribes minted their own coins, which means that everyone trusted them. Nevertheless, they were not used on an everyday level before the time of the Romans, but more like gifts (perhaps as a hoard buried in the ground as an offering to a god) or as a tribute to a neighbouring tribe.

Language

If you are going to trade, you have to use some kind of common language. In the time of the ancient Britons, it is quite likely that people spoke a range of local dialects based on a common language which spread to Britain, perhaps as early as the Stone Age. It is the language we now call Celtic.

When the Romans invaded, at the end of the Iron Age, it was likely that the ancient Britons continued to speak the ancient Celtic language amongst themselves and only spoke Latin when they had dealings with the Romans. The Britons trading east to the lands of the Saxons, may also have spoken 'Saxon', and Saxon traders may also have lived along the south east coast of Britain in Roman times.

Iron Age religion and sacrifice

Iron Age Britons had a religion that connected to nature. They didn't need burials or tombs. But they sometimes needed sacrifice.

The Romans wrote almost nothing about the religion of the ancient Britons. So what we know has to come from the things we dig up (archaeological remains).

There are almost no Iron Age tombs and few cremations, so we have to imagine that it was the custom to leave the dead to be eaten by animals – and so be returned to nature.

There are no big stone circles, only small shrines where people worshipped. So we have to assume that to Iron Age Britons, the gods were everywhere, close to the farm, in streams and rivers, and in the sky.

Celtic Art

A form of art with curving patterns spread from western Europe around 450 BC. Britons developed their own versions of the style, reserving it for metal objects such as torcs, shields (picture ② page 42) and mirrors. This style is sometimes called Celtic Art.

Offerings to the gods

Just as in the Bronze Age (pages 18–19), Iron Age British finds are nearly all magnificent items of war – shields, swords (picture ④ page 43) and daggers of great craftsmanship. They were found in the bogs of fens, in river and lake bed muds.

▶ ① **Lindow man was found in 1984 at Lindow Moss bog in north-west England. He died between AD 20 and 90. He was about 25 years of age, around 168 cm tall and weighed 60–65 kg. He had probably done very little hard, manual work, because his finger nails were well manicured. His beard and moustache had been cut by a pair of shears. His last meal probably included unleavened bread made from wheat and barley, cooked over a fire on which heather had been burnt.**

But the man met a horrific death. He was struck on the top of his head twice with a heavy object. He also received a vicious blow in the back which broke one of his ribs. He had a thin cord tied around his neck which was used to strangle him and break his neck. By now he was probably dead, but then his throat was cut. Finally, he was placed face down in a pond in the bog. This may well have been a sacrifice carried out by Druids.

Other works of art, such as torcs and chariot harnesses, were buried in special holes in the ground (picture ③ page 43). None of these items were ever used. From this we can tell that they were intended as offerings to the gods. Some unused everyday items, such as pots, querns and farm tools, are also found buried near houses, so presumably these everyday items were also offered to the gods.

People worshipped by giving things that were precious to them and the best they could make – weapons to the water god, and torcs and household goods to the earth god.

Druids

Much of British religion was controlled by a group of people called Druids. They became very powerful in Iron Age times. They acted as priests, conducting services at hillfort shrines, in lakeside shrines, in groves of trees and at springs.

It seems that if the gods were angry – perhaps there had been a drought or flood – the Druids commanded that special offering was needed – a human sacrifice! The man found at Lindow Moss (picture ①) was probably a human sacrifice made in a bog.

The Romans certainly knew of the Druids and the shrines that they controlled, for many Roman temples were built right over them in an effort to rid the country of the influence of Druids. The Roman baths at Bath were built over one such ancient spring-side shrine.

◄ ② This is probably the most famous item ever to have been found from the Iron Age in Britain. It is called the Battersea Shield because it was found in the muds of the River Thames at Battersea, London. It was probably made just to be offered to the gods and placed in the river between 350 and 50 BC, where it remained until found last century.

It was made of thin bronze covering a wooden back and then decorated with red glass and curving shapes of bronze that were of a style copied from designs of continental Celts.

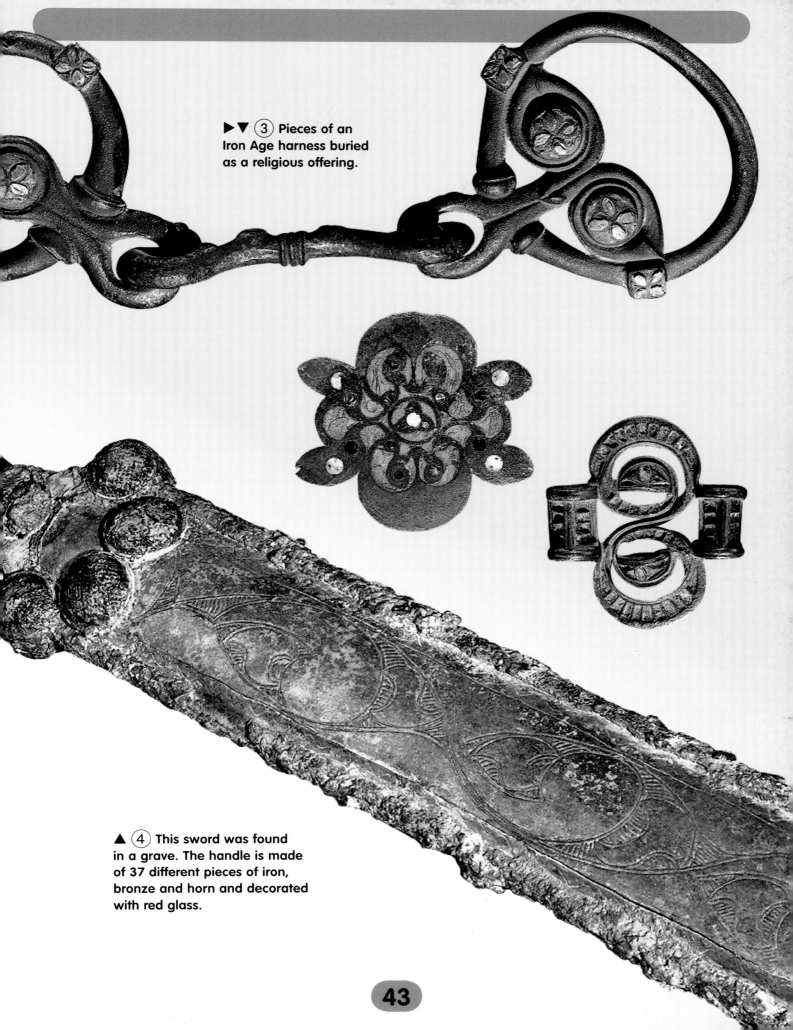

▶▼ ③ Pieces of an Iron Age harness buried as a religious offering.

▲ ④ This sword was found in a grave. The handle is made of 37 different pieces of iron, bronze and horn and decorated with red glass.

The Romans and war

The ancient Britons were forced into war with the Romans.

The Romans ignored the Britons for hundreds of years. We were on the edge of their world and useful for supplying iron, grain, wool and other things. But then the Romans conquered the Gauls (who lived in what is now France), which left Britain next in line.

How were the Britons organised?

During the Iron Age, British kingdoms had become increasingly organised. The largest were led by kings and a special warrior class – nobles (picture ①). Women could fight alongside men as warriors and could even lead whole peoples (hence Queen Boudicca who led the revolt of the Iceni people against the Romans in AD 60).

Arguments between tribes were mostly small scale and often involved just the warriors. Warfare was mainly for honour or sport, and consisted of raids and hunting. However, some kingdoms became ambitious to have more land. Some kings lost out – and they went to ask for help from Rome – just the excuse the Romans had been waiting for.

Battle tactics

Britons went in to battle wearing war paint (blue dye made from woad and painted after the Celtic Art style). Some thought they were more frightening clad in nothing but the dye and a torc around their necks.

Their way of fighting was to stand in front of the opposing army and scream and beat their

◀ ① This is what a British chieftain may have looked like. The most fearsome British weapons were long spears and a long, heavy sword. Most British soldiers did not have as good armour as this.

spears and swords against their shields. They then ran headlong into the opposing army, screaming the entire way (picture ②). This often had the effect of scaring the opposing soldiers who broke into a run. Fighting a fleeing army is relatively easy work.

In battle the Britons whirled their swords above their heads, slashing the air from side to side, then struck downwards at their enemies as if chopping wood. It was a use of the sword that terrified their enemies.

Note: The time of the Romans in England, Scotland and Wales is described in the Curriculum Visions book *'The Romans in Britain'*. But the Romans never reached Ireland at all and had very little influence on Scotland.

The screaming was all part of a plan, not because they were an unorganised rabble. However, large British armies were made of peoples from many kingdoms, so they were not experienced at being united in battle – unlike the Romans.

Caesar and Claudius

Emperor Julius Caesar attacked from the coast of Kent in 55 BC. The Romans had full-time trained professional soldiers. They had tactics to deal with an on-rushing enemy. Nevertheless, the Britons were not an easy foe and Julius Caesar was probably glad to take some hostages (the common thing to do to secure peace in those days) and retreat back to Europe. However, a century later the army of Emperor Claudius came in more strength and overwhelmed the British. That is when the Iron Age ended.

▼ ② A skirmish between the Roman army and the British.

▲ ① The arrival of the Saxons in the middle of the 5th century.

The British survive

What happened to the British after the Romans left? Did they retreat to Wales? Were they all killed by invading Saxons? Or did they just absorb newcomers as they always had?

The Romans left in AD 410 and left the Britons without an army. The Picts from Scotland and the Irish Scotti (Scots) from the west took advantage of the departure to raid into the undefended north of England. The Angles, Saxons, Jutes (shortened to 'Saxons' below) and others came in from the east (picture ①).

But there were about two million people living in 'England and Wales'. The new 'invaders' could not kill off all of these people. Neither could they force them to retreat to Wales. After all, that would mean that the Britons who retreated to Wales would be more than the modern population! No, the Britons survived. But much about their way of life and language did not.

What happened?

First of all, even two million people do not fill up England and Wales. Large areas were still uncleared of forest and other areas not farmed as closely as we would today.

▲ ② The arrival of the Vikings at the end of the 8th century.

So there was room for more people. Also many of the Britons in the south had been trading with the Saxons for hundreds of years and may well have spoken a form of Saxon even in Roman times. Many of the soldiers in the Roman army were also actually 'Saxons'.

When the Romans left, the Britons asked the Saxons to come and help keep out the Picts and the Scotti – in exchange for land. So, although there may well have been raids and skirmishes, when more Saxons came and settled, there was plenty of room, and many might well have simply enlarged British villages.

There is more on the Anglo-Saxons and Vikings in the Curriculum Visions books 'Anglo-Saxon raiders and settlers' and 'Viking raiders and settlers'.

Place names change

During Saxon times place names changed to Saxon ones. It tells us that a new group of people were now in control, with a new language. But for this to happen it simply needed Saxon nobles to defeat British nobles. Once they had taken control, the Saxons could impose their own language, their own ways, houses, fashions and beliefs.

What does seem certain is that the ordinary British survived, as they always had, and our genes prove it. The British simply took on new ways. Later on, of course, there is no doubt that Saxon England was attacked by Vikings (picture ②). But, of course, our Stone Age ancestors came from the north, so they were really distant relatives after all!

Weblink: www.CurriculumVisions.com

Glossary

ADZE A kind of axe, but with the blade at right angles to an axe blade. It was used like a chisel to shape wood.

ANCESTORS People from whom we are descended and who lived a long time ago.

BRITONS, ANCIENT BRITONS The people who lived in the British Isles before (and after) the Romans.

BRONZE AGE The time between 2200 BC and 800 BC when the main metal for making tools was bronze. The Bronze Age followed the Stone Age.

CELTIC, CELTS A word that relates to the tribe of people called the Celts who lived in part of what is now France. However, the word Celtic (as in Celtic Art and Celtic language) refers to a type of art and language that is found over a large part of western Europe (including the British Isles) and which was shared by Celts and other people. Celtic people as such never came to Britain in large numbers, although they would have traded with the British and that is how the art and language spread.

CELTIC ART A style of painting, and design used by many people of Western Europe during the Iron Age. It consisted of many swirling (natural) shapes and may have reflected the ideas of nature that were part of their religion.

CORACLE A small and lightweight round boat made of a frame of branches over which a hide was drawn tightly. The hide was made waterproof by rubbing fats in to it.

DAUB A mixture of mud, animal dung, hay, straw and water (and often many other things as well) that was mixed into a kind of plaster and spread on wattle fences to make a windproof wall. It was not weatherproof and had to be protected by wide roof eaves.

HUNTER-GATHERERS People who rely on getting food from the world around them without trying to farm. They mostly eat whatever is in season from wild plants, and catch wild animals wherever they can. This kind of life cannot support many people because most things that grow are inedible for people.

IRON AGE A time, starting in Britain about 800 BC (2,800 years ago) in which iron became the main metal for making tools. In Britain, archaeologists mark the end of Iron Age times whenever Britain was invaded (Roman invasions in England and Wales, Vikings in the Northern Isles and Ireland). This stop date is just for convenience and does not mark any real, immediate change for the way of life of the majority of people.

QUERN A pair of stones used for grinding cereal grains to make flour.

TORC A neckband made of metal.

TRIBE, KINGDOM A group of people who share the same beliefs and who regard themselves as being connected, perhaps by ancestors, perhaps by simply being in one part of the world. Another word for tribe is clan. When the area of a dominant tribe is large and governed by a ruler, such as a king, it may be called a kingdom.

WATTLE Thick, flexible branches that can be woven together to make a kind of fence.

Index